Great Big Animals

JUMBO BLUE WHALES

By Francis MacIntire

Please visit our website, www.garethstevens.com. For a free color catalog of all our high-quality books, call toll free 1-800-542-2595 or fax 1-877-542-2596.

Cataloging-in-Publication Data

Names: MacIntire, Francis.
Title: Jumbo blue whales / Francis MacIntire.
Description: New York : Gareth Stevens Publishing, 2018. | Series: Great big animals | Includes index.
Identifiers: ISBN 9781538209073 (pbk.) | ISBN 9781538209097 (library bound) | ISBN 9781538209080 (6 pack)
Subjects: LCSH: Blue whale–Juvenile literature.
Classification: LCC QL737.C424 M33 2018 | DDC 599.5′248–dc23

First Edition

Published in 2018 by
Gareth Stevens Publishing
111 East 14th Street, Suite 349
New York, NY 10003

Editor: Kate Mikoley
Designer: Sarah Liddell

Photo credits: Cover, pp. 1, 5, 7 Franco Banfi/WaterFrame/Getty Images; pp. 9, 13 Mark Carwardine/Photolibrary/Getty Images; p. 11 Andrew Sutton/Shutterstock.com; p. 15 Joe Morris 917/Shutterstock.com; p. 17 Kobac/Wikimedia Commons; pp. 19, 24 (pod) Flip Nicklin/Minden Pictures/Minden Pictures/Getty Images; p. 21 Richard Herrmann/Minden Pictures/Minden Pictures/Getty Images; pp. 23, 24 (krill) Allexxandar/Shutterstock.com.

Printed in the United States of America

CPSIA compliance information: Batch #CW18GS: For further information contact Gareth Stevens, New York, New York at 1-800-542-2595.

Contents

Blue whales are so big!

They are the largest animals on Earth.

They grow more than
100 feet long.

Some are very old. Some live more than 100 years!

Babies are big, too.
They are 25 feet long!

They live in the sea.

They swim all over the world.

They can live
in groups.
This is a pod.

They need lots of food.

They eat very
small animals.
These are called krill.

Words to Know

krill

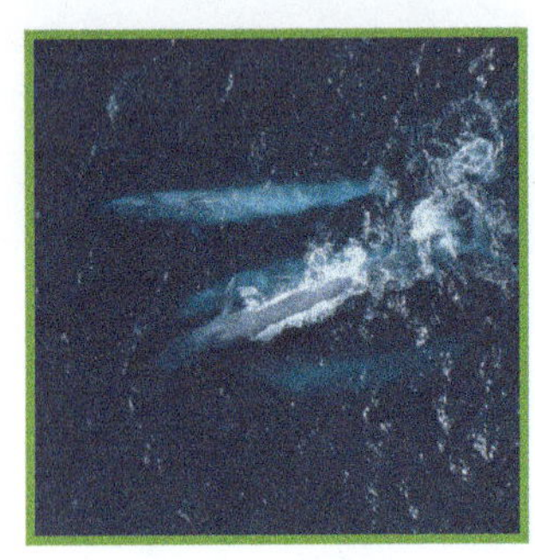

pod

Index